The Scottish Forester

John Davies

JOHN DAVIES, B.Sc., F.Ins.For., is Conservator of Forests for the South of Scotland. After war service as a pilot in the R.A.F. he went to the University of Edinburgh and graduated in 1949. The following year he joined the Forestry Commission in Wales. In 1958 he was transferred to Scotland and later became Conservator for West Scotland.

He lives near Thornhill in Dumfriesshire and is a keen naturalist, hill-walker and fisherman. At present he is engaged on re-editing the Journals of David Douglas, the great Scottish plant explorer.

THE
SCOTTISH
FORESTER

John Davies

WILLIAM BLACKWOOD
1979

First published in 1979 by
William Blackwood & Sons Ltd
32 Thistle Street
Edinburgh EH2 1HA
Scotland

ISBN 0 85158 130 7

Printed at the Press of
the Publisher

Contents

Illustrations

Illustration credits:

    ★ *Forestry Commission*
    † *Adam Collection, D. C. Thomson & Co Ltd*
    ‡ *K. H. C. Taylor, A.R.P.S.*
    § *Wiggins Teape Paper Ltd*

Preface

When Blackwood's asked me to write a short popular book on Scottish forestry, I readily assented. But, as I came to assemble the material, I became increasingly uneasy. In the first place I was aware of the scrutiny that it would receive from my professional colleagues. Secondly, there was the ever-growing conviction that I could not do justice to the great achievements of the past sixty years. Future historians and geographers are bound to note this extraordinary renaissance and must find my account far too superficial for their purposes. There are all too many omissions and over-simplifications and I know now that there is room for 'another damned thick square book', as the Duke of Gloucester put it.

Many people have helped me. I should particularly like to thank my wife for typing the book, and Graham Jeffrey and Mike Locke for invaluable advice.

For my wife, and the other long-suffering wives of Scotland's foresters.

"Believe me, the forest as an idea and as a physical and pervasive influence has been with me all my conscious life. . . . Yours, gentlemen, is one of the most honourable professions"—Sir Frank Fraser Darling, D.Sc., Ph.D. Address to the Tenth Commonwealth Forestry Conference, United Kingdom, 1974.

The Destruction of the Old Caledonian Forest

A mere twenty thousand years ago—a very short time in the earth's history—Scotland lay under a great ice-cap, in some places thousands of feet thick. Gradually the ice retreated, and about eight thousand years ago the English Channel was cut, our coastline began to define itself and the last glaciers disappeared.

The raw landscape that the ice left was rapidly colonised by the plants and shrubs one finds nowadays in the Arctic—the tundra species such as dwarf birch, dryas and arctic willow.

These were succeeded by scrubby trees which, as the land warmed up, were in turn replaced on the lower, sheltered ground by dense woodland. In this chilly wilderness a few hunters lived—very few, perhaps not more than a hundred, or, as one archaeologist has put it, 'as many as could decently get on a double-decker bus'.

Five thousand years ago, when the Eastern Mediterranean had already developed great cultures and civilisations, Scotland was still a wilderness of rugged mountains, vast forests and huge marshes inhabited by not more than ten thousand Stone Age men. Probably about sixty per cent of the land surface was under some sort of tree cover.

During the last fifty years botanists have developed a method of dating and unravelling the past, based upon pollen analysis. Briefly, the pollen of each species of plant is particular to that species and is almost indestructible by bacterial action. Pollen is released in huge quantities by plants and falls into marshes or peaty areas and is overlaid by later peat and vegetation. By taking specimens from various depths in peat bogs we can discover what the vegetation was like thousands of years ago. We also learn from these analyses that there were considerable changes in climate over the last ten thousand years. These changes, and man himself,

1

have been the greatest influences on the plant life. Nevertheless, a certain basic pattern emerges, which has a number of regional variations.

The prehistoric Caledonian Forest consisted of oak, hazel, wych elm and alder on the fertile lower slopes, which gave way to juniper, birch and pine as one went up the hillside. Above two thousand feet the pine and birch faded out, and on the summits of the highest hills above three thousand feet one found, as one does today, an alpine flora.

It had one important difference from the neighbouring European forests: by some freak Britain had only three coniferous species when the continental land connection was severed—juniper, yew and Scots pine. Silver fir, larch and Norway spruce, which were abundant in Europe, were missing and were introduced by man only within the past four hundred years.

Five thousand years ago man shared the land with several other large mammals—aurochs, wild horses, brown bears, beavers, wild boars, lynxes, wolves, reindeer and elks—which he has since exterminated. At that time man was part of a balanced system, preyed on and preying on the fellow-creatures of his environment. He tended to live outwith the forest, with its attendant perils, for his tools and weapons were made of horn, stone and bone and gave him little protection.

Man first began to make inroads into the old Caledonian Forest at the end of Neolithic times—perhaps about four thousand years ago—when Abraham was living in Ur of the Chaldees. Stone Age implements became more efficient—flint axes were perfected and a sort of shifting cultivation came to be practised. Timber was used for building, for fuel and for making enclosures. The process accelerated in the Bronze Age, and the Beaker Folk started to settle the land permanently and to clear the more open forest areas—often at the upper edge of the forest, where regrowth was slow and where grazing animals could keep it down. Man's use of fire became more sophisticated and this enabled further clearances to be made.

The Bronze Age gave way to the Iron Age and the settlement continued. It was the period of the northern brochs and the vitrified forts. Iron Age man used birch, pine and oak for smelting—an additional call on the native forest. Most of the settlements were along the coasts or in the southern part of Scotland where tree cover was less dense and more easily reduced.

By the time the Romans came to Britain, forests still covered about half of Scotland's land area. Strabo's reference to our forebears is worth quoting: 'Forests are their cities; for having enclosed an ample place with felled trees, they make themselves huts therein and lodge their cattle, though not for any long continuance.'

The Romans certainly speeded up the destruction of the forests. Pliny records probably the first Roman expedition into Scotland about A.D. 50, 'which was carried by the armed forces of Rome to a point not beyond the neighbourhood of the Caledonian Forest'—perhaps near Stirling. Around A.D. 81 Agricola made three expeditions into Scotland—to Galloway, to Fife, and to Perthshire. In A.D. 120 Hadrian's Wall was built, followed twenty years later by the Antonine Wall, linking the Forth to the Clyde. Between these walls and beyond the Antonine Wall a series of forts and outposts were constructed which finally reached up to the edge of the Moray Firth. The forts were connected by roads, and as these frequently had to cross deep bogs, a great number of trees were cut to give bottoming to the upper metal. This ancient method of road building, called 'corduroy', is used to this day. To prevent ambushes the Romans sometimes cleared woods adjacent to the roads.

Early man, then, cut the forest to provide himself with fuel, grazing and housing-timber. By Roman times, wood was being used for implements, smelting, fencing and road construction, and the forest was recognised as a resource as well as a source of danger. The population rose dramatically under Roman occupation, as it did all over Europe, and in Scotland the extent of forest shrank to about 40 per cent of the land surface.

Then came the Roman collapse—and the population of Europe was decimated by plague, economic disaster and disorder. Some authorities say that it was reduced from thirty million to a mere three million in the Dark Ages. The Scottish population probably reflected this dramatic decline and one would have expected the forests to increase again. That they did not do so is something of a mystery, and the key probably lies in climatic changes. Huge areas of once-thriving Scots pine forest had slowly succumbed to peat and may have been unable to regenerate. Deer and other grazing animals were also able to take advantage of many forsaken clearances, thus preventing regrowth.

Old pine roots exposed by peat cutting at Lettoch, Glen Livet

Although records for the six hundred years following the demise of Rome are scarce, we know that the Norsemen valued Scottish pine and oak for building their magnificent ships, and we also know that as the population started to increase again further incursions were made into the forests.

The development of sheep farming in the Borders played a significant part. Dr Corner, writing some years ago in *Scottish Forestry* on the history of land use in the Borders, explained that this was due to the creation of monastic establishments during the reign of David I in the twelfth century. The Cistercians and Benedictines were given large estates by the Crown and founded abbeys at Melrose, Dryburgh, Kelso, Jedburgh and Coldingham.

'Intensive agriculture was practised on the monastic estates. The monks were pioneers in new ideas and organisation. Forests and marshes were reclaimed and drained, arable land was enclosed, run-rig was abolished and a form of rotation of crops was practised in which the land was rested in grass and then cropped. Sheep were introduced in large numbers on the low ground and hill farming was practised on the Cheviot and Lammermuir hills. About the year 1250 Melrose Abbey had 12,000 breeding sheep. . . .'

This intensive grazing was very profitable. Forest cover was quickly reduced, and the process spread rapidly northwards up the east coast and on the drier central areas, gathering momentum all the while.

Five hundred years ago the only substantial tracts of the old Caledonian Forest lay north of the Highland Line, and inroads were made wherever access could be found. Oak and birch went for smelting, and one can find on many a scrubby or barren sloping hillside in the Western Highlands today little flat terraces, the remains of old charcoal hearths.

Great areas were destroyed in the seventeenth century to reduce the wolf population and to deny cover to outlaws. Oak and pine were cut for shipbuilding, and the particular value of old Scots pine for masts and spars was recognised long before the Napoleonic Wars. Only in the most remote places did substantial remnants remain. In 1724 Daniel Defoe in his tour of Scotland noted:

'On the most inland parts of this country, especially in the Shire of Ross, they have vast woods of fir trees, not planted or set by men's hands, but growing wild and undirected, otherwise than as nature planted and nourished them up, by the additional help of time, nay, of ages. Here are woods reaching from ten to fifteen and twenty miles in length, and proportioned in breadth, in which there are firs, if we may believe the inhabitants, large enough to make masts for the biggest ships in the Navy Royal and which are rendered of no use merely for want of convenience of water carriage to bring them away. . . .'

The settlement after the '45 and General Wade's roads made further exploitation inevitable. The following factors are well documented: the increase in Highland population owing to the introduction of the potato, vaccination and the ending of tribal warfare; the subsequent clearances of men and trees for sheep husbandry; frequent sale of timber to English merchants. All that remained were rubbishy trees with bad form and no commercial value—a genetic as well as a physical disaster.

Place-names tell their own story. Loch Goosey in Wigtownshire is derived from *Guisach*—Gaelic for a pinewood. There have been no native pinewoods in Wigtownshire for centuries. The village of Furnace, south of Inveraray on the shores of Loch Fyne, used to be called Inverleckan. In 1754 a Lancashire company erected a smelting works there. Iron ore was brought in by boat, smelted with locally produced charcoal, and the place was rechristened Furnace. In 1788, 700 tons of pig iron were produced. There was also a tan-bark industry. All over Scotland in the eighteenth century the ancient woods were being cut, and when Dr Johnson made his celebrated tour in 1773 he remarked pungently that 'a tree in Scotland was as rare as a horse in Venice'.

Ingenious ways were found for making log ponds and floating the timber down to the sea. Civil engineers like Telford built canals, harbours and roads, and finally the railway age arrived.

Railways needed sleepers, and the old Caledonian pines,

hard and durable, were excellent. But perhaps even more serious were the fires that sparks from the steam engines caused. Particularly in Strathspey, great damage was caused to the old woods by railway fires.

Thankfully there are still some small tracts of the old Caledonian Forest left, chiefly in Deeside, Speyside and Perthshire, and in some of the remote glens of the north (see page 8). Many of them are very open and straggly, like the few pathetic trees at the head of Glenfalloch near Crianlarich, but foresters and naturalists alike regard these last survivors as tremendously important.

The larger areas have an atmosphere which is unique. Partly it is the nature of the trees themselves, for they are very beautiful in their own right—flat crowned, a blueness about their foliage and the glorious red stems. Even the names of some of the forests—Affric, Amat, Ballochbuie, Mar, Glentanar, Rannoch, Conaglen, Rothiemurchus— have a certain music.

Nearly fifty years ago, when I was a small boy, I had the good fortune to come under the influence of an inspired teacher of natural history, and he stirred my imagination. I had been brought up in open country on the southern out-skirts of London, but he taught me to collect moths and butterflies and I began to read about the Highlands and the moors of the north. John Buchan had an influence too, of course, as he did with many of my generation, and the child that was nurtured under the wide skies of southern England longed to experience the brown burns and driving rain of the west coast. But perhaps the biggest influence was a number of photographs of Rothiemurchus and the Larig Ghru that I found in a natural history magazine, taken by that old Scottish master, R. M. Adam (some of whose photographs illustrate this book). Ten years later, in wartime, when I was in my early twenties, I first walked in the Speyside pinewoods, and I realised that they fulfilled all that I had expected.

Why is it? To come down from the high tops of the Cairngorms into the shelter of Rothiemurchus and smell the pines and junipers is an experience that I have never felt

Old Caledonian pine in Glen Affric

elsewhere. Words like scent and smell seem coarse, but there is a marvellous air in the pinewoods—clean and delicate. I have felt awe and a sense of unease and prehistory on the windswept Prescelly mountains in Wales where some of Stonehenge was quarried, and I have drunk of the richness in the shadows of the great beechwoods in Sussex, but the old Speyside pinewoods satisfy me far more.

Partly, no doubt, it is their open nature—stands of dense timber are rare indeed, and many of the trees are hundreds of years old and the forest has a park-like appearance. Wildlife is remarkably rich, and because of the open nature of the woodland one has a good opportunity to see a wide variety of birds—blackgame, capercailzie, crested tits, crossbills, for example—and beasts—roe deer, red squirrels, red deer. And there are the huge ant-hills, and the many species of the heather family including bilberries and snowberries and odd rarities such as chickweed wintergreen.

Sadly, however, if left to their own devices these woods would slowly disappear. There are very few young trees and the old trees bear seed infrequently. The dense cover of heather often precludes the seedlings from establishing themselves. It needs a great deal of disturbance, such as a cloudburst causing a river to break its banks and bare the soil, to enable seed to germinate. And all too often, even when the seedlings do establish themselves, they are usually grazed out by the deer that we so enjoy watching.

Twenty years ago Professor Steven and Dr Carlisle wrote a monumental book on the native pinewoods. In the final chapter they argued for their preservation:

'First they are the authentic home of the distinctive strain of Scots Pine at the western extremity of its natural distribution. Some of these strains are already important in the forestry of Britain and other countries, and others may be in the future—hence from a practical point of view this source should be maintained. Secondly, our native pinewoods are one of the most interesting survivals of our native vegetation, with a distinctive flora and fauna. There is now general recognition in all civilised countries that such survivals should be preserved on an adequate scale and it would be a national loss if these pinewoods were to disappear. Finally they can be considered to be not the least important of the historical monuments of Scotland.'

It is pleasing to be able to end this chapter by recording that special steps are now being co-ordinated by the Forestry Commission, the Nature Conservancy and by private owners to preserve many of these woods.

The Beginnings, 1460-1919

IN the previous chapter I described how the old Caledonian Forest had been reduced and how this destruction had accelerated during Medieval times.

However, way back in the fifteenth century, when the destruction was rapidly gathering momentum, and the word forester really meant gamekeeper—one who looked after a hunting-place—the first Scottish tree cultivator emerged.

William Blair, sometimes called William the Cellarer, developed a small tree nursery at the abbey at Coupar Angus, near Perth, about the year 1460. From this nursery he supplied the abbey's tenants with broom, ash, birch, hawthorn and willow-trees to plant on their holdings.

Fifty years later, in 1504, it appears that the Crown became concerned at the loss of the nation's woodlands, for James IV passed an Act requiring every landowner to plant at least one acre of woodland 'where there are no great woods or forests'.

By the beginning of the seventeenth century a good deal of interest was being taken in the growing of Scots pine. Sir Duncan Campbell of Glenorchy established a tree nursery in 1613, and we learn that in 1621 James VI asked the Earl of Mar to send him pine seed from Upper Deeside for use in England.

But John Evelyn (1620-1706), the great diarist, is really the founder of British forestry. In 1664 he published his celebrated *Sylva*—'a discourse on forest trees and the propagation of timber in His Majesty's dominions'. This was an instant best-seller and in the preface to the second edition, which was dedicated to the King, Evelyn wrote: '. . . this is to acquaint Your Majesty that it has been the sole occasion of furnishing your almost exhausted Dominions with more than two millions of timber trees; besides infinite others which have been propagated within the three Nations at the

11

instigation and by the direction of this work . . .'. He had certainly obtained Scots pine seed, for he wrote: 'In Scotland (as we noted) there is a most beautiful sort of fir growing upon the mountains; of which from the late Marquis of Argyll, I had sent me some seeds which I have sown with tolerable success; and I prefer them before any other because they grow both very erect, and fixing themselves stoutly, need little or no support.'

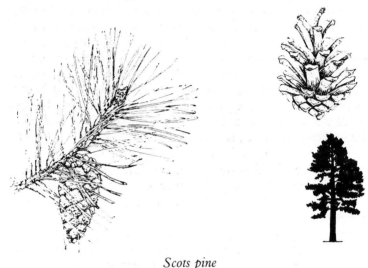

Scots pine

Evelyn's influence on the development of forestry was profound. He saw the value of woodland as a national resource and as a way of beautifying the landscape. He made the practice of forestry civilised and fashionable and stimulated a great interest south of the Border. After the Act of Union in 1707 and the ensuing stability and increase of wealth in the eighteenth century, Scottish lairds emulated their English cousins and started tree-planting on their newly enclosed estates. Thus in 1724 Daniel Defoe was able to note:

'You hardly see a gentleman's House, as you pass the Louthians towards Edinburgh, but they are distinguished by groves and walks of fir trees about them. In a few years Scotland will not need to send to Norway for timber or deal, but will have sufficient of her own and perhaps be able to furnish England with considerable quantities.'

And again:

'Posterity will find the Sweet of this Passion for Planting, which is so happily spread among the people of the South parts of Scotland, and which, if it goes on, will in time make Scotland a second Norway for fir, for the Lowlands as well as the Highlands, will be overspread with Timber. Improvements are already of 50 to 70 and 80 years standing as at Melvil, Leslly, Yester, Pinkey, Newbattle and several other Places, and others follow apace, so that in 40 or 50 Years more, as slow growing Wood as Firr is, yet there may be a quantity of large grown Trees to be found to begin upon, so as to cut out Deal-boards in large Numbers, besides Sparrs, Bauks, Poles, Oars & which the Branches will supply.'

Larch, which had been introduced into England about 1620, was brought to Scotland, and a few trees planted at Lee Park, Lanark, some fifty years later still survive. These predate the famous Dunkeld larches which many foresters believe to be the earliest trees of this species to be planted in Scotland. In fact, the first Dunkeld trees arrived in 1727 with some orange-trees for the glasshouse, and in 1737 John Menzies of Culdars (who owned most of Glenlyon) received a further consignment of trees, five of which were planted at Dunkeld, eleven at Blair Castle and five at Monzie Castle. Only one of the Dunkeld larches is still standing, but nine remain at Blair and two at Monzie.

The importance of the Dunkeld larches is that they bore seed early and fathered some wonderful specimens, one of which was recorded in 1970 as being 131 feet high, with a clear bole of 90 feet. On the evidence, larch clearly had a great future in Scotland, and 'Planting John', the 4th Duke of Atholl, started making extensive plantations up the Tay

13

European larch

valley. A most enthusiastic forester, he is credited with planting 10,000 acres during his lifetime. One nice legend about him survives. Craigie Barns, the precipitous rock face above Dunkeld, was too steep and dangerous to plant by hand. The Duke therefore ordered a cannon to be brought up so that a canister of larch seed could be fired at the cliff. A few trees grew successfully from this violent beginning.

By the mid-eighteenth century, although the old natural forest was being continually reduced, many policy woods were being made and new species introduced. Norway spruce, beech, oak and sycamore were widely planted, for they had done well in parts of England and were European species. The common Silver fir, *Abies alba*—which is so important on the Continent—was also used. There is still a 1680 tree at Dawyck near Peebles. In fact a very ancient Silver fir at Inveraray, now moribund, once held the record for being the tallest tree in Britain (180 feet), and contained over seventy-five tons of timber. Sadly, in later years, the cultivation of *Abies alba* ran into difficulties and it is hardly ever planted nowadays.

The old Statistical Accounts of Scotland, written by parish ministers, bear ample evidence of the new interest in planting. In Wigtown, the Earl of Galloway planted up to 200,000 trees a year in the last decade of the eighteenth century. Even

14

in Sutherland large pinewoods were created, and there are records of small plantings in Orkney and Shetland, albeit unsuccessful.

In the third quarter of the eighteenth century, we get the first clear evidence of the felling and thinning of man-made plantations. G. M. Trevelyan, referring to the resurgence of Scotland after the '45, writes: 'The lifting of the pressure of dire poverty from the bulk of the population, and of penury from the higher classes, set the Scottish spirit free for its greatest achievements.' This was certainly reflected in land management, for between 1750 and 1850, half a million acres were planted in Scotland. Landowners vied with each other in the excellence of their woods and started to look far afield for new species to introduce. In England numerous nurseries had been established, and the founding of what later became the Royal Horticultural Society gave an additional spur to development. Rare species were imported from all over the known world, and new introductions became important to the best nurserymen.

A remarkable race of Scottish plant collectors sprang up of whom David Douglas was the most important. Douglas was born in 1798, the son of a mason employed on the Scone Estate. He left school at the age of eleven and became an apprentice gardener. An exceptionally keen young naturalist, after a spell at Valleyfield, Fife, in Sir Robert Preston's

Norway spruce

15

service, where he gained glasshouse experience, he managed to get a job at the Botanic Gardens in Glasgow. Here he came to the notice of William Hooker, the great botanist who was later to transform Kew. Hooker took David botanising in the Highlands and helped him greatly. In 1823 the Secretary of the Horticultural Society in London asked Hooker if he could recommend someone to become a plant collector. Douglas was appointed and was sent to the eastern states of America. He brought back many new trees and plants, and his trip was voted such a success that in 1824 he was sent out again, this time to the Columbia River country in the north-west of the country. In three years he covered over eight thousand miles on horse or foot or by canoe and collected and sent back to Britain over two hundred new species of plants and trees. He kept a Journal in which he recorded his adventures in the great wilderness of Oregon, Washington and British Columbia. It was a hard life and the Indians, sometimes hostile, held the whip hand. Food was often scarce, and bears were numerous. Douglas returned home across the Rockies to Hudson Bay. He was the first man ever to ascend one of the northern Rockies, and was clearly incredibly tough. On 21st May 1827, for example, he travelled forty-three miles without food, and swam and crossed numerous streams.

On his return home, Douglas found himself famous. But he was bored and unhappy until, in 1829, he managed to get sent back again to continue his explorations. In 1831 he procured the seed of Sitka spruce. He commented: 'It possesses one great advantage by growing to a very large size on the Northern declivities of the mountain in apparently poor, thin, damp soils; and even in rocky places, where there is scarcely a sufficiency of earth to cover the horizontal wide-spreading roots, their growth is so far from being retarded that they exceed one hundred feet high and eight feet in circumference. This unquestionably has great claims on our consideration as it would thrive in such places in Britain where even Scots Pine finds no shelter. It would become a useful and large tree.' How right he was! This species more than any other revolutionised British forestry, as we shall see later.

David Douglas never returned to Britain. He conceived the idea of walking back through Alaska, Siberia and Russia, but failing eyesight and the unsettled state of the countries prevented him. He met his end tragically in Hawaii in 1834, when he slipped into a pit built to trap wild cattle, and was gored to death by a bull.

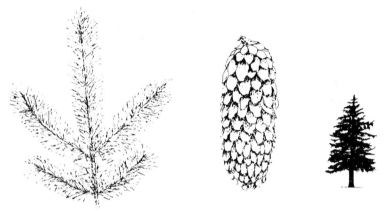

Sitka spruce

Before Douglas's introductions, the British forester had a limited range of conifers at his command: Scots pine, a slow-growing tree, European Silver fir, Norway spruce, European larch and Corsican pine. None of these trees can stand exposure really well and only one, Scots pine, can tolerate very poor soils. Douglas introduced three important Silver firs: the Noble fir (*Abies procera*), one of the loveliest of all trees, the Grand fir (*Abies grandis*) and *Abies amabilis*. He also introduced six new species of pine, including *Pinus radiata* (the Monterey pine), which has been used all over the world, Douglas fir and of course Sitka spruce. All the Silver firs, Sitka spruce and Douglas firs are fast-growing, high-yielding species, and Sitka and *Abies procera* have the precious advantage of being able to grow well in very windy conditions. It was little wonder that the horticultural world was greatly excited by Douglas's discoveries. Even small gardens that cannot accommodate his great trees are richer by his introductions, for he brought back the flowering currant, Clarkia, and *Lupinus polyphyllus* which, crossed with *Lupinus arboreus*, has given us those glorious Russell lupins.

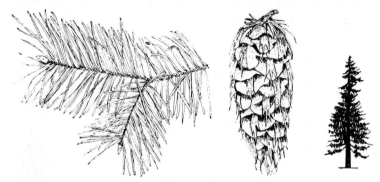

Douglas fir

In 1850 a group of Scotsmen decided to send another plant collector into the Douglas country. They formed the Oregon Association and chose a certain John Jeffrey, a native of Forneth in Perthshire, for the mission. Like Douglas he proved to be a tough traveller. In a letter dated April 1851, written at Jasper House, on the edge of the Rockies, he described his journey from Hudson Bay: 'The distance from Cumberland House to Jasper House is 1200 miles. During this journey I slept with no other covering than that found under the friendly pine, for the space of 47 nights, on several occasions the thermometer standing from 30° to 40° below zero.'

Jeffrey sent back some ten parcels of seeds as well as many plants and is credited with the first introductions of *Abies magnifica*, *Tsuga heterophylla*—Western hemlock—and Lodgepole pine (*Pinus contorta*), a species which has been extensively planted on the sourest peats during the past thirty years. John Jeffrey never returned to Britain and probably met a violent death in the Colorado country in 1854.

During Victorian times the plant collectors were very busy. China, Japan, the Himalayas and the remote mountain areas of the Americas were scoured. However, despite all the introductions of that period, only seven coniferous trees are extensively used in Scotland—Sitka spruce, Douglas fir, Norway spruce, Scots pine, European larch, Japanese larch and Lodgepole pine. And of these, in the words of the good book, the greatest is Sitka spruce.

In 1854 what is now known as the Royal Scottish Forestry Society was formed—a body which was later to play a significant and an honourable role in formulating a national forest policy. I suppose that about this time too the Scottish forester, like the Scottish gamekeeper and the Scottish engineer, emerged as a British sub-species, fostered by the royal interest in Scotland and all things Scottish!

From 1850 until the last few years of the century, however, the rate of private commercial planting slowed down. Britain had such wealth from its Empire that the need to have a forest resource of her own was not apparent. Forestry—and agriculture—fell into a period of decline. Home-grown products could not compete with products from the new lands that were being opened up. Many woodlands became valued more for their sporting potential than for their timber potential. On great estates the forester lost out to the head keeper.

Nevertheless the interest in tree-growing was maintained almost everywhere, but on a more horticultural level. Arboreta were established and a steady stream of new introductions made. Important among these was Japanese larch, brought in by J. H. Veitch and planted by the Duke of Atholl at Dunkeld in 1885. This species, more vigorous and easier to grow than European larch, has become an important part of the landscape of Scotland.

The first eleven trees were planted below Dunkeld House, on Kennel Bank, near where the progeny of the first great European larch had been established. Seed was later collected from the trees, and in 1904 it was noticed that some of the resultant seedlings had an intermediate shoot colour between the straw of European larch and the chocolate of Japanese larch. Furthermore, the trees appeared to possess remarkable vigour, and it was clear that a new species, the now famous Dunkeld hybrid larch, had been bred.

A number of far-sighted men became uneasy at the lack of commercial planting, and before the end of the century there was increasing concern about the risk of relying completely on timber imports. In response to this a series of committees and Royal Commissions were set up, and much credit should go to the Royal Highland and Agricultural Society of Scotland and to the Royal Scottish Forestry Society for continually urging the claims of a home-based industry.

The most important of the committees was the Royal Commission on Coast Erosion which reported in 1909. The original warrant was to inquire and report:

'as to the encroachment of the sea on various parts of the Coast of Great Britain—what measures are desirable for the prevention of the damage—and whether further facilities should be given for the reclamation of tidal lands'.

A later warrant was added in the following terms:

'Whether in connection with reclaimed lands or otherwise; it is desirable to make an experiment in afforestation as a means of increasing employment during periods of depression in the labour market, and if so by what authority and under what conditions such experiments should be conducted.'

The principal recommendations were that Parliamentary powers should be obtained for:

'(1) The appointment of Commissioners charged with the duty of carrying out a national scheme of afforestation.

(2) Vesting in the Commissioners powers to survey land and decide what land is suitable, and also power to acquire such land.

(3) Authorising the Treasury to grant to the Commissioners an annual free loan for the necessary period.'

The 'national scheme of afforestation' envisaged the planting of nine million acres by the State over sixty years—a most ambitious undertaking.

It is interesting to record that this huge incursion into what was traditionally a private-enterprise field in a period when private enterprise was at its strongest was widely welcomed, and the Royal Scottish Forestry Society sent a deputation of landowners to the Chancellor to urge its adoption. Included in the party were Sir Herbert Maxwell of Monreith (the grandfather of the writer Gavin Maxwell), Lord Novar and Colonel Steuart Fothringham of Murthly.

In 1911 the Society sponsored a full-scale afforestation survey of the Great Glen. This was carried out by Lord Lovat and Captain Archibald Stirling of Keir, and many eminent landowners, foresters and academics contributed their views. Their conclusions were:

'(1) The Survey of Glen Mor tends to prove that there exists in Scotland a large extent of land admirably fitted for afforestation.
(2) Under a well-framed scheme large areas of land can be afforested without serious injury to existing interests.
(3) Afforestation on the lines suggested would eventually not only pay its way but bring in a considerable return to the Forest Authority.
(4) A great deal of permanent and periodic employment would be given by the establishment of forest centres.'

In Buchan's life of Sir Walter Scott there is a memorable passage: 'In 1771 Scotland stood at the parting of the ways. That she chose rightly was due to two children who were then alive on her soil. One was a boy of twelve, the son of a

21

small farmer in Ayrshire, who was picking up an education on a moorland croft. The other was an infant in an old house in the College Wynd in Edinburgh. . . .' In a less celebrated but like manner the twentieth-century resurgence of British forestry owes much to two Scottish landowners, Simon, Lord Lovat (1871-1933) and Sir John Stirling-Maxwell of Pollock (1866-1956), who were as dissimilar in many ways as Burns and Scott, but who both had vision and deep patriotism.

Sir John Stirling-Maxwell was undoubtedly one of the greatest of all British foresters and his claim to fame rests upon his remarkable pioneering work on some of the most intractable sites in Scotland. Between 1892 and 1913 he made extensive plantations of conifers at elevations of between 1,250 and 1,700 feet at Corrour, near Loch Ossian. He tried out many different species and, most important of all, he introduced into Scotland a system of turf planting from Belgium which pointed the way to the methods that the Forestry Commission later developed and which have enabled all but the most impossible peat bogs to be effectively planted. If you take a young tree and plant it straight into a wet peat bog it may just survive, but it certainly will not grow. The Belgians had found that if you cut square blocks of peat, pull them out of the ground and set them in lines at about four-foot spacing you can plant trees on them most successfully, and even at high elevation they will grow away to form a plantation. Sir John developed and refined this method in the most extreme conditions and also pioneered the use of phosphatic fertilisers. He was by all accounts a most charming, modest man, who was a considerable water-colourist in addition to owning a marvellous collection of Spanish paintings. His kindness and enthusiasm certainly inspired many of the new generation of young foresters. Fittingly he became one of the first Forestry Commissioners when that body was set up in 1919, and from 1929 to 1932 served as Chairman.

Lord Lovat was a very different man. In his youth he had explored the Blue Nile, and had formed the Lovat Scouts which played such a significant role in the later stages of the Boer War. The *Dictionary of National Biography* says:

'Lovat's hospitable nature gave him an unrivalled power in dealing with men: his services to the British Empire as soldier and administrator—to his own countryside in promoting forestry, fisheries and the welfare of the crofter—depended largely on his capacity for getting a team to work together. That he should be its captain mattered not at all to him. To his enthusiasm and experience the Forestry Commission and the first Empire Forestry Conference held in Canada in 1923 owed everything. A staunch Roman Catholic, he formed, with men of all creeds, a host of effortless friendships. . . .'

Although he was a knowledgeable forester, Lovat was more interested in the sociological and strategic importance of forestry than in its technical problems. During the early years of the twentieth century he tirelessly lobbied his fellow peers and fellow politicians for a sensible, dynamic national forest policy. He knew that it could be the means of restoring the Highland economy and repopulating some of the empty lands.

It was due to this pressure that the Crown Office of Woods purchased the Inverliever estate on Lochaweside in 1909 and started afforestation work on the wet Argyll hills. At about this time too, the University of Edinburgh began to run courses which were later to lead to a B.Sc. in Forestry.

However, all too soon the nation became embroiled in a struggle for national survival, and during the Great War tremendous inroads were made into the forests that had been planted from 1750 onwards. Indeed so serious was the shortage of timber that many remote remnants of the old Caledonian Forest were exploited.

At the height of the war Sir Francis Acland, M.P., headed a government committee to examine means of developing the nation's forest resources. The Committee recommended that:

(1) The nation should adopt a forest policy to ensure that

there was always a strategic reserve of timber in the country sufficient to sustain a three-year war.

(2) That steps should be taken, through the forest industry, to arrest the drift from the land.

(3) That a national forest authority should be set up both to create state forests and to stimulate private forestry.

And so, by the time the war ended, the stage had been set for some real progress. It was up to the survivors to see what could be done.

National Forest Policy, 1919-78

SHORTLY after the end of the First World War, a Forestry Act was passed setting up the Forestry Authority for Great Britain. The Act was based on long-term objectives extending to fifty years and beyond and included finance for the first ten years of operation. It marked the beginning of a national forest policy, and upon it all our progress over the past sixty years has been founded.

In 1919 the scene was truly daunting. In Scotland nearly all the exploitable remnants of the old Caledonian Forest had gone, and the greater part of the half-million acres planted between 1750 and 1850 had been felled. Many of the young men who might have led a national recovery were dead and the nation was exhausted.

But the Forestry Commission came into being and Lord Lovat was appointed Chairman. Among the first Commissioners were Francis Acland, Lord Clinton, Sir John Stirling-Maxwell and the young Australian Rhodes Scholar, Roy Robinson. It was a very strong board and it needed to be. In the first year of its existence, starting from scratch, 543 acres were planted in Scotland, at a total direct cost of £13,790! In the second year tremendous progress was made—planting rose to 1,968 acres, a foresters' school was founded at Beauly, and degree and diploma courses were introduced at the Universities of Aberdeen and Edinburgh. In addition, the nucleus of a Research Branch was created and advisory services were instituted. Nine technical papers were published and a national census of woodlands was undertaken.

And then the blow fell. The Geddes Axe threatened the entire organisation. Lovat fought like a lion. The Annual Report for 1921 has this dry and illuminating note:

'The Commissioners regret the delay in the presentation

of their Second Annual Report. At the time when the Report was due to be prepared the whole future of State Forestry was in the melting pot and they were engaged in presenting afresh the national need for a forest policy. In the circumstances they felt it less urgent to report progress than to ensure that there should be progress to report.'

In fact the infant thrived and when Lord Lovat resigned in 1927, he left behind a group of dedicated men who had already started up fifty-five new Scottish forests.

The early reports of the Commissioners make good reading. They are lucid, enthusiastic and full of vision. From early times great attention was given to resettlement, and many small farms or forest-worker holdings were established, many of which have enabled men with little capital to get a foothold on the farming ladder. These holdings have been a success and the scheme has been extended. The demand for them today is perhaps stronger than ever.

During the inter-war years, the rate of afforestation was dictated purely by the vicissitudes (and they were many) of the money supply. Land was available in enormous quantities at very low prices—in the 1920s and '30s many of the Highland estates changed hands at less than £2 per acre, all in. But with agriculture in a depressed state, little private planting was done in spite of the help of a small government grant. Indeed most of the woodlands cut in 1914-18 lay derelict.

In 1932 Roy Robinson became full-time Chairman, and it is really due to him that the Service was welded into a close-knit, coherent whole. He was a tough, single-minded man, deeply respected and feared by his staff. Robinson was to the Forestry Commission what Reith was to the B.B.C., but unlike Reith he continued in the Service he had created, until his death in 1952. Not for him the sad years of underemployment when at the height of his powers.

In 1935 the Commission, acting on the advice of Sir John Stirling-Maxwell, set up a Forest Park scheme and designated a large area around Arrochar as the Argyll Forest Park.

A fine stand of fifty-year-old Norway spruce at Drummond Hill, Perthshire

This bold initiative in welcoming the general public into the countryside was way ahead of its time. Today there are four great Forest Parks in Scotland—Argyll, Galloway, Queen Elizabeth and Glenmore—covering nearly a quarter of a million acres of superb scenery. It is worth recording that Sir John's daughter, Mrs Anne Maxwell Macdonald, inherited her father's vision, for in recent years she has gifted Pollok House with its wonderful paintings and grounds, to the people of Glasgow.

It is not my intention to describe the growth of the Commission in detail, but by 1939 some 137,000 acres had been planted in Scotland, compared with 210,000 acres in England and Wales. On reflection this was rather disappointing and I feel that if Lord Lovat had lived longer he would have urged a more dynamic programme upon all concerned. He would have felt that his beloved Scotland had not fully taken up the opportunities he had fought for.

The Second World War resulted in heavy fellings in private woodlands. Almost all the remaining woods planted in the golden age between 1750 and 1850 were cut and even some parts of the old Caledonian Forest that had been spared during the First World War came under the axe. Large numbers of New Zealanders and Canadians were drafted in for this essential work, but the sacrifice was truly appalling. I remember those wholesale fellings of pinewoods in the Spey and Dee valleys particularly (opposite). The lessons of 1914-18 were rammed home and another wartime investigation was made. The report 'Post War Forest Policy' was published in 1943 and made out an almost irresistible case for a much more ambitious national planting programme.

In 1945 a new Forestry Act was passed and the Government accepted the principle that there should be five million acres of productive woodlands in Britain, which would take fifty years to establish. In order to set the ball rolling funds were made available to plant 365,000 acres in the first five years, mostly by the State.

The Forestry Commission reorganised itself and recruited trained staff from universities, forestry schools and from

Glenfeshie in 1943. Wartime felling of remnants of old Caledonian Forest

overseas. Under a London headquarters, national directorates were set up in England, Scotland and Wales. Scotland was further subdivided regionally into four conservancies—North, based on Inverness, East, based on Aberdeen, West, based on Glasgow, and South, based on Dumfries. It was a period of excitement and expansion—university training expanded, research work stepped up and an ambitious programme of rural housing started. Roy Robinson—by then Lord Robinson—who had been in at the inception of the Commission, combined the offices of Chairman and Director-General, and over the next twenty years Scotland was well served by a number of men of high ability and enthusiasm, not all of whom can be mentioned in a short book. However, James Fraser, Conservator for North Scotland, Frank Oliver, Conservator for East, and J. A. B. Macdonald, Head of Northern Research and later Conservator for South Scotland, cannot be left out. Two Directors, Sir Arthur Gosling and Sir Henry Beresford Pierse, and the two university professors, H. M. Steven and Mark Anderson, must share in the honours, together with John Dickson, who came out of the North Conservancy to become Director-General and who retired in 1977.

And so it was that these men led a great drive to recreate a real forest wealth in Scotland. How well they succeeded can be judged by the growth of the Forestry Commission's woods:

F.C. Plantations
in Scotland

Year	Acreage
1930	47,000
1945	176,000
1950	256,000
1960	560,000
1970	860,000
1975	1,079,000

These men, the leaders, were followed by many worthy and enthusiastic disciples—forest officers, engineers, land

30

agents, foresters and workers—who gave substance to their dreams and were glad to have an opportunity to do a really worthwhile job in their own countryside.

Private forestry prospered too, following the introduction of the so-called 'Dedication Scheme' which, with planting and management grants, rewarded owners who managed their woodlands properly. Instrumental in this advance have been the Scottish Woodland Owners Association, which has made skilled advice readily and cheaply available, and the Institute of Foresters, a highly professional society which maintains a list of consultants.

It is pleasing too that that stalwart body, the Royal Forestry Society, has gone from strength to strength, providing a forum for all who care for Scotland's woodlands to meet and discuss problems together, regardless of wealth or status. It publishes an excellent quarterly journal, *Scottish Forestry*, and can look back on over 120 years devoted to the well-being of Scotland's countryside.

But perhaps the most remarkable phenomenon of the post-war years has been the establishment and activity of private forestry companies. Major agricultural improvements are almost invariably fuelled from city money in the first place. For two centuries the Scottish countryside has drawn capital from outside, often from rich merchants returning to the land of their forebears. The forestry companies follow this old tradition, for they have solicited funds from the wealthy and from institutions by drawing attention to the considerable tax advantages to be gained from investing in forestry. At Eskdalemuir in Dumfriesshire, for example, the Economic Forestry Group manages some 28,000 acres, divided among forty-five owners. By the early 1970s the forestry companies were establishing thousands of acres of plantations every year. Although changes in taxation have recently reduced the scale of investment, further expansion seems likely.

All in all the last thirty years have brought a transformation in our countryside. The age-long exploitation has been arrested and Scotland now has 12 per cent of its land area back under trees, compared with 4 per cent in 1947. In some Regions, the advance has been even more spectacular. In Dumfries and Galloway, for example, the area under trees has increased from 4 per cent to 21 per cent.

The technical improvements that have been made since 1919 are too numerous to detail in the space available, but certain advances, which are of international importance, must be recorded.

Let us consider the problems that faced the pioneers sixty years ago. First, they had only three proven coniferous species at their disposal—European larch, Scots pine and Norway spruce—and none of these was happy in an exposed position. The second factor, wind, has a fundamental effect on the life and landscape of Scotland. The west coast is one of the windiest places on earth—almost in the same league as Tierra del Fuego and the southern tip of New Zealand. During the thirteen years that records were kept at the observatory on the summit of Ben Nevis, there was an average of 263 gales per annum exceeding 50 m.p.h.! The tree-line may be only a few hundred feet above sea-level on the coast, and in very few places can trees grow reasonably above 1,500 feet. Compare this with the Alps, where the tree-line is sometimes about 8,000 feet, and it will be seen that this problem, which still causes difficulty, was particularly daunting to the pioneers.

And then there was the quality of the soil. Many of the soils of upland Scotland are infertile, acid and waterlogged. Foresters are always talking about 'plantable land'. In their jargon it means land which is too poor for intensive agriculture but will grow an economic crop of trees. 'Unplantable land' means land that is too poor to grow an economic timber crop. It may be too rocky, too steep, too wet, too infertile or too exposed, or a combination of these factors. To the Commissioners in 1919 vast areas of upland Scotland fell into the 'unplantable' category. And yet Lovat and his associates saw a real challenge in the bad lands, for if they could be properly afforested, the rural economy of some of the most impoverished areas of Scotland would be transformed. They

32

decided to plant what they could on the good land, thousands of acres of which was cheaply available, and to start long-term investigations on sites of the poorest types.

The chief of these types was peatland. Peat is formed by plant remains which cannot break down properly because of waterlogging or high rainfall. Peatlands started to form in Scotland some 7,000 years ago as a result of climatic change, and at the present time over 10 per cent of the country's land surface is covered by peat, twelve inches or more in depth—over two million acres in fact. Sixty per cent of Caithness, 32 per cent of Sutherland and 25 per cent of Wigtown are peat covered, and there is a peat moss near Falkirk which is over forty feet deep. Many of the deep peats have no agricultural value and in their present state are incapable of growing more than deer grass, heather and sphagnum moss. Trees planted directly into them languish and often eventually die.

In 1920 a small Research Branch was set up, and H. M. Steven was appointed Research Officer for Scotland. Steven, who later became Professor of Forestry at Aberdeen, was a brilliant choice. He had been greatly impressed by Sir John Stirling-Maxwell's work at Corrour and set to work to see if the peats of Scotland could be made to grow trees economically. The Corrour work had shown that trees could be established on peatlands if planted out on large turves and treated with phosphate, but costs were prohibitive and growth was very slow. As the research work progressed, the size of the problem seemed to grow too. Peats varied in acidity, in consistency, in depth and in fertility. M. L. Anderson, who followed Steven on peat development (and later became Professor of Forestry at Edinburgh), realised that if only the land could be ploughed the site would be improved. In 1927 and '28 attempts were made to pull a plough by horses, but they failed. Laboriously, by hand, mock furrows were cut and planted, so that the trees were surrounded by turves on all but the drain sides. This method, although very costly, showed a great deal of promise. Nevertheless, until the peats could be ploughed mechanically, the work was uneconomic. Crawler tractors with low load-bearing capacities were still not available, so research was concentrated on testing different tree species, on drainage work and on experimenting with fertilisers. It was found among other things that Lodgepole pine would grow on very infertile peat, but that the more valuable Sitka spruce was much more difficult to cultivate.

At last, in 1939, one of the new crawler tractors became available, and for the first time mechanical cultivation was possible. An area was ploughed at Borgie, in the far north in Strathnaver, and planted with Japanese larch, Sitka spruce and Lodgepole pine. Tragically the whole area, which was growing well, was destroyed by fire in 1942 and it was not until 1944 that the work could be resumed.

During the 1940s, crawler tractors were more readily available, and with their increased power and low weight-loadings per square inch of track, they were able to cross all but the wettest bogs. Commission staff began to design special forest ploughs for the tractors in order to drain the peatlands and provide turves for planting. One of the first ploughs was designed by Davie Ross, the Commission's forester at Minard in Argyll, a highly original and remarkable man. James Cuthbertson, the agricultural engineer of Biggar, further developed Ross's ideas, and by the late 1940s it was clear that at last most of the great peatlands of Scotland could be cheaply drained and cultivated mechanically for tree-planting. It was a tremendous breakthrough. Cuthbertson's ploughs, developed for Scottish forestry conditions, have been used the world over. A little later, the Clarks at Parkgate, near Dumfries, started to develop dry-ground ploughs and have evolved a remarkable range of specialist forest-ploughing equipment which has also been widely exported. There are now forest ploughs which can drain quaking bogs or shatter iron pans and indurated layers of soil two feet below the surface, thus greatly increasing the land's potential (opposite). The contributions of Scottish inventors to world forestry are considerable. And certainly the huge planting programmes that were undertaken in the early 1970s within Scotland could never have been com-

34

pleted without the machines that Cuthbertson and the Clarks evolved in association with Forestry Commission staff.

A modern forestry plough

A few years ago I climbed Ben More Assynt. It had been raining heavily for two days, but when I reached the summit the rain had stopped and it was crystal clear and utterly still. I recall lighting my pipe and seeing the smoke rise vertically. Away to the north my eye travelled over mile after mile of gleaming rock and peat bog, across to Ben Hope and Ben Loyal, and in the north-east I could see the sun shining on the Pentland Firth and the distant outline of Hoy in the Orkneys. The little inn at Crask and its few green fields fifteen miles away stood out in the huge brown wilderness. It was a scene of unforgettable magnificence, a cruel landscape, utterly inhospitable and bereft of cover. And I reflected that it was scenes like this that had provided a challenge to the early Commission foresters.

Some of the feelings of the old pioneers and their excitements and disappointments come through in a recent letter I had from John Dickson, who retired from the Service last year after holding the post of Director-General. Much of his working life was spent in the north. He writes:

'There is an interesting story of how our standards have changed. In 1919 Professor Borthwick of Aberdeen University, as Technical Adviser to the Commission, surveyed Borgie [in Strath Naver, Sutherland]. He said 5,000 acres were plantable. In 1932 a survey of the areas planted amounting to 1,071 acres led to the belief that only about 400 acres would succeed. Shortly before the outbreak of war, another survey was done and then only 1,000 acres were deemed plantable. In 1942 the whole of Borgie, bar a dozen acres, was burned down. After the war still only 1,000 acres were deemed plantable with ploughing (as was then). In 1951 I got hell from James Fraser for daring to plant 200 acres of the failed area. By 1974 about 5,000 acres had been successfully planted and were growing well. Borgie had a chequered history. It was largely a Lodgepole pine subject and Lord Robinson would not let us import such seed. So any oddment we could collect from our own trees was welcome, but the origins were all wrong and we were in such a hurry that seedlings were often used. Success was dreadful. Sitka was used much more than should have been but it succeeded very little even after two or three doses of fertiliser on experimental areas. Of course ploughing was not all that good. I for one was very despondent about Borgie. At best it was a moth-eaten forest. It was not until a visit probably 4 to 5 years ago that I got a surprise and said, "By God, we have got a forest at long last here."

'Rightly or wrongly I have been given the credit for venturing into this arena and reclaiming, in Fraser Darling's words, "the wastes of Sutherland, Caithness and

36

Ross-shire". This decision was based on the Research Plots in Strathy and Watten laid down in 1949-1953 or so. From these it was evident by the early '60s that one could grow crops which were almost certain to reach utilisable size. There was a risk that they could not but they had grown well for 13 or 14 years and looked healthy so the risk seemed minimal—so in we went.'

The development of successful afforestation techniques for the peatland areas of Scotland, whether it be on the great moors of Caithness and Sutherland, the sour mosses of West Lothian or the flows of Wigtownshire, is something in which we can take pride.

Jonathan Swift put it well in *Gulliver's Travels*:

'And he gave it for his opinion, that whosoever could make two ears of corn, or two blades of grass, to grow upon a spot of ground where only one grew before, would deserve better of mankind, and do more for his country than the whole race of politicians put together.'

The Forestry Process

MOST of the new forests that have been created since the war have been planted on poor hill-grazing land, for the fertile 'brown earth' soils have nearly all been reclaimed and are under intensive agriculture. This explains why most of the new forests are coniferous, for conifers are usually far more tolerant of poor soils than hardwoods such as oak or beech. With 12 per cent of Scotland's land surface under trees compared with 4 per cent in 1947, and a current planting programme of around 60,000 acres, people may well ask how much more can be planted. Recent surveys indicate that there are just over six million acres of land suitable for planting, of which 2,200,000 acres are already afforested. It would not be possible to plant the balance without a substantial loss to agricultural production and amenity, but by the end of the century, foresters hope that the forest area will have increased to about four million acres. Relations between hill farmers and foresters are becoming increasingly cordial, for each side appreciates more fully the needs and aspirations of the other, and the benefits that can accrue from co-operation. Integration is no longer a catch-phrase. Hill farms can often be redesigned to allow substantial areas for trees, and the money made available from this can finance big farm-improvement schemes, to say nothing of the benefits of shelter, fencing and mutual roading. Four million acres of well-managed woodland producing five million tons of timber a year in fifty years' time—what a marvellous national investment that would be!

Townspeople visiting the countryside seldom appreciate how technical the modern process of afforestation is, or how much hard work and planning is carried out before a single tree is put in the ground. First of all, if the plantation is to be of any size, the owner must get permission to plant it from the Forestry Commission. This is to stop valuable food-producing land or land of great landscape value being lost. The Forestry Commission consults with the Department of Agriculture for Scotland and perhaps with the local planning officer before giving its decision. If permission is given, the area will be eligible for grant aid.

The next step is to survey the soil types in the planting area and to draw up a 'choice of species' map, together with cultivation and fertilisation plans. As we have seen, the forester nowadays has considerable power to improve a site by cultivation, drainage and fertilisation relatively cheaply. And he is aware of this as he comes to decide what plants to order from the forest nursery.

If the site is conspicuous, the good forester will try to make his new planting beautiful as well as productive and will use hardwoods on the richer sites and larches on prominent knolls and along roadsides in the knowledge that they will give a blessed diversity of colour and habitat. He will also consider the shape of his new plantation to ensure that hard straight edges are avoided wherever possible and that it sits gently in the surrounding landscape and does not obtrude.

Also at this stage, if the woodland is to be a large one, he will survey future forest road lines and divide the area up into 'compartments' of about twenty-five acres, separated by roads or rides. These compartments serve as management units or 'geographical addresses' within the wood and are needed in order to describe accurately where work is to be carried out.

The area is next fenced against stock and, in red deer country, against deer, and cultivated by huge crawler-drawn ploughs which throw up great turves at two- or three-metre spacing. This cultivation ploughing improves the drainage, aerates the soil allowing it to weather and release nutrients, but above all provides an excellent weed-free planting medium for the young trees. After cultivation the area is often 'cross-drained' by even bigger ploughs, in order to lead surplus water off the hill and assist in further drying out of the site. Very few species of tree can tolerate waterlogged conditions and the wise forester wishes his trees to be able to root deeply, thus enabling the crop to withstand gales.

In some places the land may be too steep to plough, and on such sites the forester may cut and spread turves—rather like Sir John Stirling-Maxwell did at Corrour—or, if the soil is rich and well drained, plant directly into it.

Now for the planting. Nearly all the trees used in Scotland are grown in special forest nurseries and great strides have been made since the war in improving nursery techniques, so that today our forest nurseries are among the best in the world (opposite).

Just as in farming, the quality of the stock is vital, and we have learned a lot about genetics and the characteristics of some of the strains and varieties of the main species we use in British forestry. The forester pays great attention to what he calls the 'provenance' or origin of the tree seed. Lodgepole pine is a case in point. It is native to the western seaboard of Central and North America, from Mexico to Alaska, and therefore grows under a wide range of conditions. In Scotland it has been shown all too clearly that seed from only a very few of the provenances is likely to be successful.

In order to ensure that only the best seed is used 'seed orchards' have been established for certain species such as larch and pine, and tree breeders have been hybridising and selecting good strains as a matter of prime importance.

Conifer seed are often very small—there are nearly 300,000 Sitka spruce seeds to the pound—and they are sown broadcast in raised seed beds in the spring. In the following spring the seedlings—usually some two or three inches high—are lifted and transplanted in lines by machines adapted from the cabbage planter. After a further year or so in these lines, which are kept as weed free as possible, the trees are lifted, graded, tied into bundles of fifty or a hundred and sent to the planting site. Modern nursery methods are so efficient that the young trees—each about twelve inches high—cost only about £20 per thousand.

Now comes the great rush. Every year in Scotland, between February and May, some sixty million young trees are planted on our hills. The work is almost all done by hand, for

Fleet Nursery. Millions of small firs ready for planting

attempts to mechanise planting have so far failed. It is hard, exacting work and we and our children owe a debt to the devoted men who have created our great new Scottish forests, working high up in the hills in the cruel spring winds. The planter invariably uses a special spade and carries a large planting bag which contains up to a hundred transplants. On ploughed ground he walks alongside the turf ribbon and plants his trees about six or eight feet apart in the upturned turf. A good planter can put in over a thousand trees a day on reasonable land.

Planting

After planting, the area may be lightly fertilised using coarsely ground rock phosphate, or, on deep sour peats, a mixture of rock phosphate and muriate of potash. In the old days this was put on by hand, but it was unpleasant, tedious work, and now helicopters are usually employed to spread the fertiliser.

Some tree species such as Sitka spruce take readily, but

others—Corsican pine is an obvious example—do not transplant well and sometimes die mysteriously. The forester fears a prolonged spring drought, for he knows that he may have losses which will require costly replacement or 'beating up' in the following spring.

The new wood needs a good deal of attention during the next few years, before it is properly established. Weeds must be kept in check, and the young trees must be protected from fire and from grazing by rabbits, hares, deer and sheep. Sometimes the grass growth becomes so dense that it encourages voles to multiply, and these little animals can create havoc, particularly in plague years. Zoologists believe that they tend to increase perhaps on a seven-year cycle, and if the plantation is made on a grassy site and the vole cycle is coming to a peak they can eat out their natural food and then destroy the young trees. Indeed in the 1950s in mid-Wales I once saw hawthorn hedges stripped of their bark by a plague of voles.

After four or five years the trees are, or should be, well established, and a quiescent period starts as far as the forester is concerned. Every now and then drains are checked and more fertiliser is applied, but the young wood normally needs little attention for the next ten or fifteen years.

Within the wood itself, however, fundamental changes are taking place. The trees grow about eighteen inches a year, slowly knitting together and killing most of the vegetation. Animal and bird populations change, foxes increase, as do roe deer; but hares and rabbits decrease, except on the edges, for their food has disappeared. The wood becomes almost impenetrable to man—an area of dense cover.

If all has gone well, after twenty years the trees will be about thirty feet high and the plantation ready to give its first yield of thinnings. About a third of the crop is removed to give the rest room to grow. The forester attempts to favour vigorous well-shaped trees and to even out the spacings. The trees to come out are marked and measured and felled and then taken to the roadside where they are cross cut and stacked to await delivery to the customer (see page 44).

Extracting logs to roadside

The first thinning usually yields only chipwood, pulpwood, pitwood or fencing timber. Thinning is usually repeated at five-yearly intervals, however, and the second and subsequent thinnings provide an ever-increasing proportion of saw logs, which are more valuable. Thinnings represent the first income that the owner can realise after twenty or thirty years of investment. At the present time, because of the immaturity of most of Scotland's forests, only about 50 per cent of the production finds its way into sawmills. Most of the remaining 'small roundwood' goes into pulp mills to make paper and cardboard. Chipwood mills (sometimes called particle board mills) take about 5 per cent of the gross production, and pitwood and fencing material together account for a similar proportion.

In Scotland, most trees are clear felled at around fifty years of age, then the ground is quickly replanted and the cycle starts again, perhaps using a different species, or a better strain of the same species.

Written like this, the whole process seems so simple, but there is a constant effort to improve techniques and productivity. A few years ago it was shown that productivity was rising by about 5 per cent per annum, compound. This has been achieved by employing work-study techniques, by bringing the results of research quickly into general management practices, and by keeping in close touch with developments in agriculture and forestry abroad.

If great advances have been made in the planting of waste land by cultivation and fertilising, and in sorting out the best species and strains to grow, daunting problems lie ahead and these will be discussed later.

Those who work in forestry in Scotland can be divided into three main groups: forest workers or woodmen; technically trained foresters who are usually in charge of a forest or part of one; and professional foresters—usually graduates—who are in charge of groups of forests.

The forest workers are usually, but not invariably, countrymen. Upon their broad shoulders rests much of the physical work that forestry entails. They do the fencing, planting and weeding. They fell the timber, extract and cross cut it. It is a tough job, but great strides have been made in the last twenty years to mechanise the heaviest jobs and to train and equip the men to higher standards. Craft courses are run and certificates are issued. Skill is being increasingly recognised and paid for, and piecework schemes are widely employed.

Technical and professional foresters are both subject to lengthy training before they are qualified. During my thirty-odd years as a professional forester I must have interviewed and advised hundreds of boys who are 'keen on forestry'. Many of them come from urban surroundings and almost invariably they reply to my opening question "Why do you want to be a forester?" with the remark that they do not want an office job. As the interview proceeds, I find out about their tastes and their interests and try to explain that the job entails long hours, a sense of responsibility and

The final dividend. Clear felling

frequent physical discomfort. I must also explain that competition for jobs is keen and that the financial rewards, even at the top, are not particularly attractive. If the boy is still interested, I often try to fix him up with a holiday job so that he can experience some of the monotony and unpleasantness of draining or weeding, and the ferocious habits of the Scottish midge. Many of the youngsters who stick it out this far go on to get the necessary experience and qualifications for the Foresters' Training School or university. If one doubts the qualities of the younger generation, one need only interview boys who are interested in forestry. They are remarkably diverse and enterprising, and my experience is that the successful ones usually have, or quickly develop, a pronounced sense of vocation.

It usually takes four years or so before a lad is qualified, and if he applies to the Forestry Commission for a job he has to pass a competitive interview and serve a probationary year or so before his appointment is confirmed.

What of the forester's year? Some of the work is of course seasonal, but unlike the work of the farmer or the nurseryman, harvesting goes on throughout the entire year. Trees are cut, extracted and dispatched to pulp mills and sawmills from January to December—if the weather allows.

The protection of the forest is also a continuous activity. Rangers have to be instructed to keep sheep out, to keep roe and red deer under control and rabbit and fox populations down. Each task has its particular season, and the additional hazards of moorburn in the spring can cause our man much anxiety. Inspection and maintenance of march fences takes up the slack—in a big scattered forest there may be a hundred miles of fencing.

The most pressing work occurs in the first six months of the year. During the long winter days following Hogmanay the forester is making sure that the land he will plant in the spring is properly prepared. In his jargon this is called 'prep ground'. It involves fencing, ploughing and draining, and it must all be ready before the young plants are dispatched by the nursery.

As the days lengthen the nursery becomes a hive of activity. Plants are lifted, counted, bundled and stored, seed beds are prepared and last year's seedlings are transplanted to give them strong root systems.

If there is a spell of open weather early in March the forester will call for the delivery of the plants, and the planting season gets under way. From now on he is under great pressure, for he may have to get a million or so young trees into the ground before the end of May. He cannot plant in frost, or in very dry weather, and the care of the little trees before they are planted is a constant worry.

Once the planting is over he can relax a little, but weeding soon starts and nitrogenous and potassic fertilisers have to be applied by midsummer.

In late summer/early autumn he starts planning the following year's work: laying out roads and rides; discussing drainage and ploughing patterns; deciding on fence lines; choosing the best species of trees to plant. By September these programmes will be under way and he will be checking quality and quantities of work, and examining plantings to see if they need attention. Quality control is vital in a long-term business like forestry. If a car manufacturer sells a badly designed component it shows up quickly and can be replaced. A forester, on the other hand, lives with his mistakes for a lifetime!

But it is a satisfying, full life. The forester may live in a remote glen, where, inside and outside working hours he will have to face a bewildering variety of problems, technical and human, from organising a mountain rescue to coping with a serious accident or sudden flood. And he will mark the passage of the seasons and have time to reflect on the individuality of mankind and on his own contribution to the landscape.

It is not surprising that foresters are a highly original lot. A. G. Macdonell wrote: 'Those whose lives are occupied in combating the eccentricities of God regard as very small beer the eccentricities of Man.'

The New Forests

I have explained why the forests planted since 1919 have, of necessity, been almost entirely coniferous, and why, with only one commercial conifer—Scots pine—left to us after the last ice age, introduced species have predominated. In fact Sitka spruce, the importance of which David Douglas recognised 150 years ago, is now the most widely planted tree. Its high-volume production, fine timber and ability to withstand exposure have been recognised.

If you look at a modern forestry map of Scotland (see pages 50-51) you will notice that most of the forests have been planted on the upper areas of the west and centre, in the zone of higher rainfall. This is because they were the least profitable for hill farming. Some of the names, incidentally, are puzzling. In the early days forests were often called after the property which the Commission had bought, but as adjacent areas were acquired the original names became inappropriate, amalgamations were made for management reasons and more suitable regional names chosen. For example, Borgie Forest near Bettyhill became part of Naver Forest.

Although the new forests have made a tremendous impact on the landscape, the change in the wildlife has been even more dramatic. Fraser Darling and others have pointed out that the bare upland landscape we had come to love—in R. L. Stevenson's words, 'Hills of sheep and the howes of the silent vanished races'—was in fact a devastated countryside, bereft of cover.

In 1920 Professor Ritchie wrote his authoritative book *The Influence of Man on Wildlife in Scotland*, a fascinating account of disastrous losses to our fauna following the destruction of the woodland. Reindeer, elks, wolves, brown bears, lynxes, wild boars, beavers, bustards, cranes and polecats have all gone. Ritchie examined the status of some of the survivors—wild-cats, pine-martens, red deer, roe deer and

49

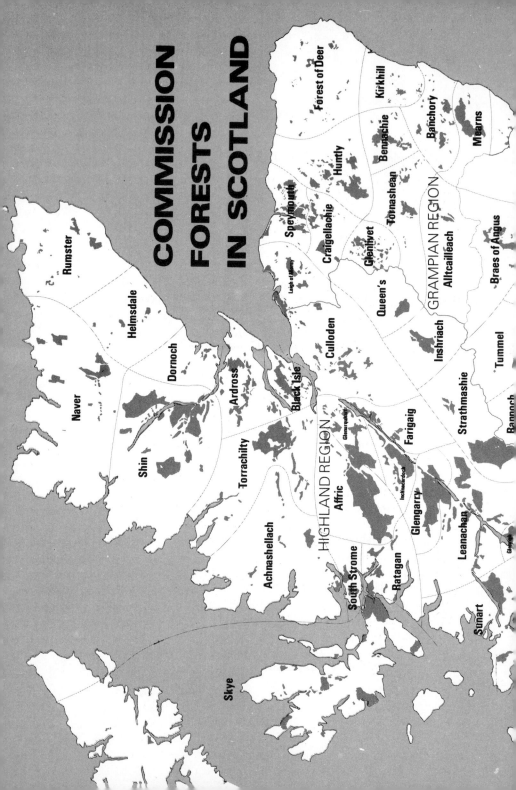

COMMISSION
FORESTS
IN SCOTLAND

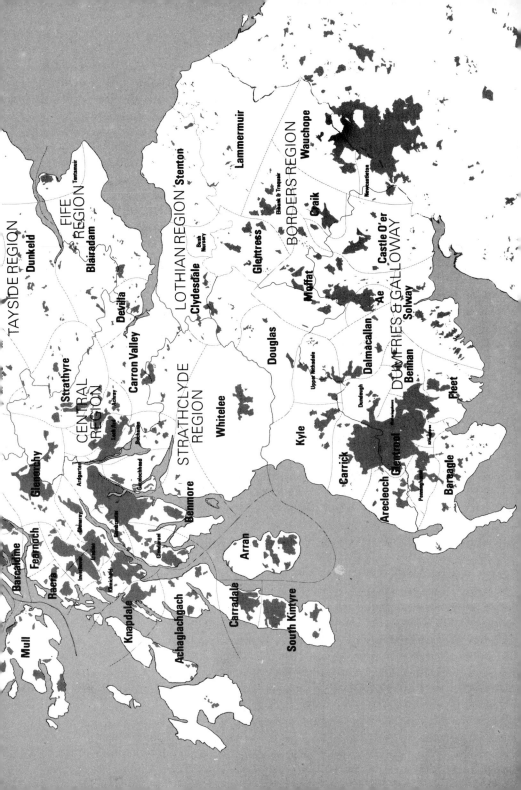

red squirrels—and in all cases found their range greatly restricted compared with former times, and, in the case of the deer, reduced in quality also. He doubted whether wild-cats and pine-martens would survive.

Naturally he could not foresee the massive planting programmes of the next sixty years. The result has been the restoration of cover on an unprecedented scale, and the effect on the native fauna has been wonderful. The wild-cat is a good case in point. Ritchie wrote: 'Since 1880 the wild-cat in Scotland has proceeded rapidly upon the path of extermination and there is little likelihood of its ever regaining lost ground outwith those fastnesses in the forests of Wester Ross and Sutherland, of Inverness and Argyll, to which it has been driven by the hand of man.' How different today! Wild-cats are now quite common in the Highlands and have come back down into the Lowland belt from which they have been absent for over 100 years. I well remember the excitement we felt in the 1960s when we found them breeding in Carron Valley Forest, outside Falkirk. I have no doubt that they will continue to move south, taking advantage of the new woods that have been made in Lanarkshire, and return to the Southern Uplands and the great Galloway forests by the end of the century.

Pine-martens too, once confined to the north-west Highlands, have multiplied and spread down the Great Glen. They have already reached the Mull of Kintyre and will surely consolidate their position right across the Highlands; though whether they will be able to cross the Lowland belt to the southern forests is open to doubt.

Red deer have increased their numbers and range greatly. In 1977 there were 270,000 in Scotland, compared with 160,000 in 1965—six times more than in the whole of West Germany. They are really woodland animals which took to the high tops out of necessity and lost size in so doing. The new wild herd which has colonised the Galloway forests consists of magnificent animals, often more akin to the ancient red deer of Britain in weight and antler size than the present-day Highland deer.

A fine young roebuck

Nobody knows how many roe deer there are in Scotland, but everyone who lives on the edge of the country sees them frequently. When I worked in the Commission's offices in the centre of Glasgow I received numerous calls for advice from folk in Bearsden, Kilmacolm and Newton Mearns whose roses were being eaten by roe deer. There are certainly far more than there were twenty years ago, and in some places they are becoming, for all their elegance, something of a pest.

Deer, foxes, badgers and martens have all found the new cover that the forests have provided much to their liking. And so have the birds. In an article in *Birds* the organ of the R.S.P.B.—Peter Hope Jones gave the following table:

		Habitat			
	Grazed moorland	Sitka woodland			
		Up to 1m high	1-3m	3-10m	10-25m
Dominant bird species	Meadow pipit Skylark (grassland) Grouse (heather)	Meadow pipit Skylark Whinchat	Willow warbler Robin Wren	Robin Wren Goldcrest	Goldcrest Coal tit Chaffinch
Total bird density (Pairs per 100 acres)	20	30	60	80	100

This increase was borne out by a recent survey in the Forest of Ae, Dumfriesshire, which showed that the population of songbirds in uniform spruce forest was of the order of 500 pairs per square kilometre—far more than on adjacent open moorland sites.

One particularly lovely bird, the hen harrier (opposite), was nearly extinct at the beginning of the century. In a recent book on the subject, the famous ornithologist Donald Watson attributes much of its recovery—there are perhaps 500 pairs in Scotland at present—to afforestation.

54

Hen harrier. A species which has benefited immensely from forestry operations

Many foresters are keen naturalists and the Forestry Commission has been able to conserve and protect many rare species through the activities of its rangers. There are many instances of eagles, harriers and peregrines owing their survival to the vigilance of the humble men who work in forestry.

In addition to creating cover for our wildlife, the new forests have provided thousands of miles of 'edges'. "Always look at the edges of things, boy," my old teacher used to say. "The edge of the wood—the edge of the moor—the edge of the barley field—even dusk and dawn, and certainly the seashore and the side of the loch—these are the places to watch."

The landscaping of some of the Commission's early plantings was not always felicitous. A lot depended on the local staff, for Lord Robinson paid little attention to visual appeal.

He was concerned solely with establishing as much productive woodland as possible with very limited resources. Some of the plantings in the 1920s and '30s were straight-lined and sat uneasily on the landscape. One thinks of the forests in the Cowal district of Argyll and the blocks at Balquhidder in Perthshire. But here and there some very lovely plantings were done: the Duke's Road area near Aberfoyle; Strathyre, where the son of Sir John Stirling-Maxwell's old forester at Corrour, Alasdair Cameron, made a most beautiful forest; and Knapdale in Argyll, which owed much to Sir Arthur Gosling. Private planting varied too, but the work of the late Duke of Buccleuch on his great estates in the south of Scotland has seldom, if ever, been equalled. Wren's epitaph, *'Si monumentum requiris, circumspice'*—'If you would see his monument, look around'—comes to mind.

The appointment of the famous landscape architect Dame Sylvia Crowe as consultant to the Forestry Commission in the early 1960s marked a turning-point. Her modest and sensible approach charmed everyone and made foresters aware of their responsibilities.

The planning of the recently designated Queen's Way in Galloway is a good example (opposite). On this twelve-mile stretch of road between New Galloway and Newton Stewart planting started some forty years ago and has continued intermittently until now. In 1973 it was decided to draw up a long-term landscape plan for the road. Photographs were taken, sketches made, in all seasons. Planting lines were pegged out, changed and changed again, and finally the whole concept was surveyed and put on paper. Queen's Way is certainly a far more interesting road to travel than it was a couple of years ago, and the eye is constantly encouraged to explore fresh vistas. I should like to see it in thirty years' time, if only to learn from our mistakes.

Landscape leads on to recreation. It will be recalled that in 1935 Sir John Stirling-Maxwell was instrumental in designating certain areas as Forest Parks and encouraging public access. Since then the use of the forests by the general public has grown apace, and the amenities provided have done a

The Queen's Way, Galloway

good deal to help the tourist industry.

There are now nine proper camp-sites scattered through Scotland, with 1,400 pitches. Other facilities include 168 forest walks and trails; fifty-two forest cabins and holiday houses; and ten information centres ranging in size from the well-appointed David Marshall Lodge at Aberfoyle to the modest little centre at Glentress, near Peebles. Pony-trekking, fishing, climbing, hill-walking, orienteering, canoeing and day-permit shooting have been developed in many forests.

In 1976, Mrs Jean Balfour, the Chairman of the Countryside Commission for Scotland, opened the Raiders' Road in Galloway—the first forest road ever to be opened to the public. The fifteen-mile stretch (for access to which one has to pay a small fee), through the huge plantations, penetrates into the heart of some very wild country, and there are some glorious picnic sites, as well as paddling pools on the River Dee where children can enjoy themselves. If one is quiet roe deer or even a red deer may be seen, and the bird life is particularly rich and exciting.

For many years, when the children were small, we camped on the Commission's site at Glenmore on the edge of Rothiemurchus Forest. There are great walks, fishing and swimming in Loch Morlich and a whole range of outside attractions. And if it rains, there is always the Aviemore Centre.

Glaswegians are fortunate to have the Queen Elizabeth Forest Park on their doorstep. The eastern shore of Loch Lomond with the oakwoods stretching down almost to the water's edge possesses great charm, particularly if there are not too many people about.

Nowadays I spend a good deal of my leisure time walking, camping and fishing in the Galloway Forest Park. It is like the Highlands in miniature, and the central area round Loch Enoch and the Merrick has an air of its own. More and more people are coming to Galloway every year—the Deer Museum at Clatteringshaws with its famous 'Galloway Window' had 50,000 visitors in 1978 compared with 20,000 in

1975—and yet one can walk for a couple of days on the high tops and not see more than a dozen folk. But there can be conflict. The rock face that is so attractive to the climber may be the nesting site of a rare bird, and the canoeist can land on an islet and disturb another scarce species. The hill-walker can knock down a dike and allow the farmer's sheep to stray. The boys camping on the edge of the forest can start a fire which they cannot control. All these things have happened in the last few years, and will happen again.

Sir John Stirling-Maxwell was a private landowner who had a vision that the State forests should, as far as possible, be made accessible to the public. His vision has been realised to a remarkable degree, and many private landowners, too, have followed this lead and opened up their woods to the public. The response has been gratifying, the losses negligible.

To quote Fraser Darling again: 'The forests of Britain are no longer remote preserves cared for by nervous men, but places where the public are invited to share an environment which I truly believe worked its magic on those who planted and tended through half a century of learning.'

Production, Progress, Problems and Prospects

AS the Scottish forester looks back over the past sixty years he cannot but feel proud of the progress that has been made in his own countryside. Let us summarise it:

(1) He has increased the area under trees from 3 per cent in 1919 to 12 per cent in 1978, and his work provides employment for over 10,000 men.

(2) He has greatly improved the rural economy by finding ways of making thriving plantations grow on useless land, particularly on the deep peats, and has developed and exported specialised machinery designed for this purpose.

(3) By the introduction of new species and by the selection of new strains of trees, he has increased the future yields of our forests and has been able to push the economic planting line hundreds of feet farther up the hill.

(4) By the judicious use of small quantities of inorganic fertilisers he has in many instances been able to stimulate normal tree growth by at least 30 per cent.

(5) He has probably saved certain species of birds and animals from extinction by restoring cover to many barren hillsides, and he has certainly increased the numbers of many other species.

(6) By opening up hundreds of thousands of acres of land to the general public and by encouraging their use of this land, he has improved the quality of life of many of his fellow-men.

(7) In other instances he has been able to beautify a dull, barren landscape.

(8) He has been able to provide the raw material for new industries, and the flow of this raw material, which doubles every ten years, should provide more wealth.

60

Perhaps we ought to consider the importance of timber production, which is after all the forester's *raison d'être*, in more detail.

At the present time Britain spends about £2,000 million annually on imported timber and timber products. Only 8 per cent comes from our own resources, whereas we produce about one-half of the food we eat. For Britain as a whole, it is clear that we shall always be heavily dependent on timber imports, and by the year 2000 we shall be doing well if we can provide 15 per cent of our needs from our own forests.

As far as Scotland is concerned, the position is much healthier, and by the end of the century she should be a net exporter. Scottish production, currently running at about 1,400,000 tons, is expected to rise steeply in the next twenty years to about twice that figure, and to rise steadily thereafter to perhaps five million tons in forty years' time, provided that we continue to plant at a reasonable rate.

Big new industries will have to be phased in, and no doubt some of the 160 sawmills at present working in the country will be modernised and enlarged and milling capacity rationalised. New timber-using industries will spring up near these new mills, often integrated within them. There are obvious advantages in adding value as close as possible to the source of production, and this should further strengthen the rural economy.

During the next twenty years it seems likely that another major pulp mill on the lines of the Fort William mill may also be needed. The Wiggins Teape mill at Fort William is a success story (see page 62). It is Britain's first integrated chemical pulp and paper mill, and the huge complex covers an area of eighty acres. Production started about fifteen years ago, and it now takes in 1,000 tons of logs a day, and can turn out 50,000 tons of paper and a further 40,000 tons of pulp a year. It has brought considerable prosperity to the Fort William district, for not only does it employ nearly 1,000 people earning good wages, but over 500 new houses have been built and it has given a lease of life to the old West Highland railway. A lot of timber is brought in by rail via the

The Fort William pulp and paper mill. The slopes of Ben Nevis in the background

loading yard at Crianlarich, and paper and pulp are dispatched by rail too. It is not surprising that other local government regions are anxious to see pulp mills established.

One of the most pleasing developments of the last few years is the way in which we have come to utilise almost the entire tree. Formerly when a log arrived at the sawmill it had to be squared and about a third of the 'slab wood' was virtually wasted. In a modern mill the log is put on a peeler to remove the bark (for which a horticultural use has been developed), then it is squared by means of a profile chipper and the chips are fed to a pulp mill or chipboard mill. The squared log is then cut up to best advantage and the return maximised by means of a computer.

Away from timber utilisation, foresters and research workers are engaged on developing new techniques all the while, and at the Northern Research Station of the Forestry Commission on the Bush Estate, south of Edinburgh, a whole range of exciting work is being undertaken. Areas of research include tree breeding and the possibility of increasing timber yields by a more sophisticated use of fertilisers. But perhaps most important are the investigations into ways of minimising wind damage.

Many problems lie ahead, some latent, some already challenging. Our forests are fairly pest free, but the incidence of Dutch elm disease and the severe damage caused by Pine Beauty moth caterpillars to Lodgepole pine plantations in the north of Scotland are warnings of the sorts of things that we and our successors will have to face. New pests and diseases will certainly arise and do great damage until they are brought under control.

If I were to choose three particularly complex problems which will be with us for many years, I would select timber harvesting, depredation caused by red deer and wind damage.

Twenty years ago plantations ready for first thinning were usually 'brashed' up to six feet—that is, the dead side branches were sawn off by hand, and trees marked and cut. The thinnings were dragged out by horses. It was very hard work—both on men and horses, particularly in steep, broken country—and often very expensive. In order to reduce costs and relieve men of the appalling labour of this type of work, machinery was introduced. Plantations suffered a bit, for the machinery needed room and large gaps had to be cut to accommodate it. Sometimes the wind got in and blew down further trees. Machinery becomes more expensive and complex and there seems to be a real danger of the forest being designed round the machine rather than the machine round the forest. In Scandinavia, Canada and the United States, where labour costs are very high, huge machines have been built which drive into the wood, grip the tree, shear it off its root, lift it up, remove all the branches and cross cut it in little more time than it takes to read this page. These heavy machines, however, may well do great damage to the soils of the forest by compaction. Thus it is possible that overenthusiastic mechanisation could bring grave perils to the forests we have laboured so hard to create.

The second problem relates to the huge increase in the red deer population in the Highlands since the last war. The restoration of cover and the absence of the deer's natural predator, the wolf, are two factors. Red deer can do a terrible amount of damage to trees; deer fencing is not always effective and is expensive to erect and maintain. And once deer get into a big forest they are the very devil to get out.

The third and most obstinate problem is wind. In the words of Saint John, 'The wind bloweth where it listeth, and thou hearest the sound thereof, but canst not tell whence it cometh, and whither it goeth.' We have managed to find species which can tolerate wind—Sitka spruce being outstanding—and which will continue to grow in severe exposure, but we cannot always get them to remain standing after attaining a certain height. Sitka spruce, for example, is unable to root deeply on some of our more intractable upland soils and is liable to be blown over before it reaches fifty feet. Much original work is being put into this problem. Contoured models have been built in plaster and polystyrene and subjected to airflows in wind tunnels. In several instances these models have enabled us to predict windthrow with remarkable accuracy.

But research workers are short of basic data; there is a lack of meteorological stations taking wind measurements in the hill country. An ingenious, cheap and effective method has been evolved using 'tatter flags' made of a standard material which slowly wastes away in the wind. The greater the exposure, the faster the wastage or tatter. This method of measuring exposure is believed to have originated in Orkney when forest research staff were investigating the possibilities of tree planting on those windswept islands. They heard the story of a local doctor who, at the beginning of the century, wanted to find a sheltered spot on which to build his home. He bought lots of penny flags and set them out on his land; then he built his house on the site where the flags were least worn.

Soil type and exposure are key factors, but there is still a great deal to be learned before we can predict with confidence how tall the trees will grow on many of our hills. The nub of the problem is this: the taller they grow, the more unstable they become; and yet the taller they grow, the more valuable they are. And just to add to the problem, once every fifteen or twenty years some part of Scotland is subject to a great storm, a master storm, and if it lasts for more than a few hours, it will bring down almost everything in its path (see page 66). Nevertheless, most Continental foresters envy us our mild, oceanic weather, for we are able to grow timber far faster than they can.

We have traced the development of Scottish forestry down through the centuries, and seen how in the last half-century the process of exploitation has been halted by a number of far-sighted men. The forester tends to choose his career at an early age. He is speedily made aware that the opportunities for becoming wealthy are slender and that he may well find it difficult to practise his vocation, for jobs are scarce. What is his philosophy? Why does he think that what he is doing is so worthwhile? I have heard many arguments put forward over the years. Perhaps the best are these:

Part of Inverliever Forest following the great gale of 1968

It is thoroughly worthwhile to be restoring a natural resource for our children and their children at a time when this generation is over-exploiting almost all other natural resources, from fish to fossil fuels.

The forests that are being planted are creating wealth out of waste land. Some of the early woods made by the Commission are now being felled. Established on land which was bought for £2 of £3 per acre, for a total cost of about £20 per acre, the best of these woods are now worth £2,000 standing per acre. Even allowing for inflation, this is a great increase in wealth.

An acre of average-quality, home-grown Sitka spruce yields £10,000 worth of paper or housing timber over fifty years. Scotland's 2·2 million acres of woodland may not all be as productive as that, but they will make a sizeable contribution to the balance of payments and will help to replace oil revenues as they run out towards the end of the century.

Forestry offers an opportunity for ordinary people of widely differing abilities and gifts to make a living in the countryside, realising in the words of Sir Robert Grieve, the first Chairman of the Highlands and Islands Development Board, 'the aim of adding another perfectly possible way of life to that in the great cities'.

The Laird of Dumbiedykes's words round off the forester's philosophy: 'Ye may be aye sticking in a tree—it will be growing when ye're sleeping.'

A Few Figures

International

	% under forest	Forest per head of population (acres)
E.E.C.	22	0·30
France	26	0·61
West Germany	30	0·30
U.K.	9	0·07
England	7	0·05
Wales	11	0·25
Scotland	12	0·31

U.K.

Land surface	60 million acres
Woodland	4·8 million acres
Population (1971)	56 million
Imports (1976)	£s
Oil	5,000 million
Food	4,500 million
Timber and timber products	2,000 million
Total imports	31,000 million

Scotland

Land surface	19 million acres
Woodland	2·2 million acres
Population (1971)	5·2 million
Av. planting for five years (1972-76)	65,000 acres
Timber production (1976)	1½ million m³ (1¼ conifer; ¼ hardwoods)

Reading List

A Field Guide to the Trees of Britain and Northern Europe, Alan Mitchell (1974).

Geology and Scenery in Scotland, J. B. Whittow (1977).

The Highlands and Islands, F. Fraser Darling and J. Morton Boyd (1969).

A History of Scottish Forestry (2 vols), M. L. Anderson (1967).

The Influence of Man on Animal Life in Scotland, J. Ritchie (1920).

Lost Beasts of Britain, Anthony Dent (1974).

The Native Pinewoods of Scotland, H. M. Steven and A. Carlisle (1959).

Trees, Woods and Man, H. L. Edlin (1956).

Woodland Birds, Eric Simms (1971).

Woodlands, William Condry (1974).

The Forestry Commission, 231 Corstorphine Road, Edinburgh EH12 7AT (Tel: 031-334 0303), publishes a wide range of leaflets and books. A Publications Catalogue is available. Free leaflets include: *Forestry Commission Cabins and Holiday Houses, Forestry Commission Camping and Caravan Sites, Forestry in Scotland, See Your Forests (Scotland), Wayfaring in Your Forests.*

Among priced publications, which are available from Government Bookshops and through booksellers, the following are of particular interest: *Argyll Forest Park, Common Trees, Forests of Central and Southern Scotland, Forests of North-East Scotland, Galloway Forest Park, Glenmore Forest Park, Know Your Broadleaves, Know Your Conifers, Queen Elizabeth Forest Park.*